COREOLOGY

Six Principles for Navigating an Election Season without Losing Our Witness

Josh Ross

Copyright © by Josh Ross

All rights are reserved. This book or any portion thereof may not be reproduced or used in any manner whatsoever without the express written permission of the author except for the use of brief quotations.

No portion of the book can be photocopied or scanned for use of distribution.

Imprint: Independently published
Printed in May 2024.

ISBN: 9798325885136

All Scripture quotations, unless otherwise indicated, are taken from the Holy Bible, New International Version. Copyright ©1973, 1978, 1984, 2011 by Biblica, Inc. Used by permission of Zondervan. All rights reserved worldwide. www.zondervan.com The "NIV" and "New International Version" are trademarks registered in the United States Patent and Trademark Office by Biblica, Inc.

Front and back cover design by Caroline Chester.

Editor: Jenna King

In honor of Jim Coleman and Jim Berryman.

Two friends, mentors, and spiritual giants in my life.

These men modeled for me what it looks like to navigate sensitive topics in the local church and in culture. They believed that unity, peace, and mission can survive our many differences. They equipped me to believe that too.

CONTENTS

INTRODUCTION

CHAPTER ONE: CONFESSION   1
    I will daily confess that Jesus is the Lord of my life and nothing else is.

CHAPTER TWO: DEVOTION   19
    I will create and honor regular spiritual practices that remind me of my devotion to Jesus.

CHAPTER THREE: RESISTANCE   37
    I will resist allowing any media outlet to become the primary way I think about culture and the world.

CHAPTER FOUR: PEACEMAKING   55
    I will strive to become a peacemaker.

CHAPTER FIVE: HOSPITALITY   71
    I will practice hospitality as a way to learn, grow, and invest in other people.

CHAPTER SIX: SERVICE   87
    I will choose to regularly serve others.

Final Words   101
Acknowledgements   105
Appendix

Introduction

In the spring of 2022 Kayci and I hosted a trip to Israel. A few days before embarking on our trip, I attempted to remove six shrubs from our flowerbed in the front of the house. To my credit, I succeeded in removing the shrubs, but not without paying the price.

These shrubs had bothered us for a few years. They were hard to keep, and they kept us from being more creative with what we did with the front of our home. I decided to go after this project with nothing but a shovel and my own two hands. I don't want this to sound braggy, but I do work out a few times a week. I enjoy it. It's therapeutic for me. Yet, I don't stretch or work out in a way that reflects the motions and movements that are needed to pull out shrubs in the flowerbed.

COREOLOGY

That evening, my lower back began to spasm. The next day, I could barely walk. By the third day, I was pretty much motionless. My back was out, and a flight around the world awaited me.

I do not suffer from chronic back pain. I have tweaked my back only a few times in my life. Once, I overdid an abdominal workout. I thought it would be fun to challenge myself to do ten minutes of crunches without stopping. I got to ten, alright, but I paid the price for the next few days. The other time I tweaked my back was from turning my head while sneezing in public. Injuries like that are embarrassing. When you're injured you want the story to be that you were helping a small child out of burning car, or that you were helping a widow remove a tree from her yard after a storm rolled through.

When asked, "What happened to your back?" You don't want your response to be, "Well, I turned my head to sneeze in my elbow because it's the polite thing to do, and then, tweak!"

Yet, demolishing the shrubs was the worst I had ever tweaked my back. I was one day away from boarding a flight to Tel Aviv to lead a trip, and I could barely move. At one point, I was in the bathroom, and I noticed my balance was off a little bit. I lifted my shirt up to see my spine and I was contorted. I limped to the living room where Kayci and my two boys were sitting on the couch watching reruns of *Psych*. I stretched my arms out and asked if they noticed anything. Their immediate laughter answered my question. My youngest asked if it was a trick. Nope. It wasn't a trick. Just contorted.

Lots of stretches and muscle relaxers were my friends for the next few days. Travelers to Israel have pictures of me stretching by the Sea of Galilee, in Capernaum, on the Temple Mount, and in airports. My tweak provided comedy relief.

Upon our return to Memphis, I chose to visit a physical therapist to help make sure I'm taking good care of my back. He talked me through essential components of caring for my core. A stronger, healthier core makes for a stronger, healthier back. Our core is the central link that connects upper body and lower body. A strong core enhances balance and mobility. It's the key to having a better back. If we neglect our core, it can

COREOLOGY

result in back pain, poor posture, and all kinds of discomfort. Of course this doesn't mean that you have to have rock solid abs in order to have a healthy back for life, but it does emphasize that our core is important to overall physical health.

I'm not writing this book to increase our desire to have six packs and beach abs. I'm writing to help us take seriously how we are strengthening the core of who we are. It is the center of our existence. It is the foundation we build our lives and values upon. For those of us who have chosen to follow Jesus, it is the source of our witness to the world.

***

I'm writing this book because I am hopeful.

It's not a false hope.

It's not a manipulative hope.

It's not a reluctant hope.

It's a hope rooted in the fact that Jesus launched a group of people to be passionate witnesses in a dark world. This was Jesus's Plan A to restore a world that was broken. And Jesus had no Plan B. We have what it takes to be passionate, genuine, courageous witnesses in the world. The church has enormous potential to do so much good.

I'm also writing this book because I want the people of God to be prepared. Much of life is how we react to people, situations, and circumstances, but if one's faith is only a reactionary faith, maturity and growth can only go so far. A vibrant faith is a faith that prepares through practices, disciplines, intentionality, and strategic action.

I'm writing this book because I'm concerned about Christian witness and our credibility in the world. My concern is heightened in an election year. It can take hours, weeks, months, maybe even years for people to trust the witness of a Jesus-follower, and that witness can be blown in a moment. It can be blown with one social media post, a negative encounter, or an insensitive comment.

Hopeful. Preparation. Witness.

I am hopeful.

COREOLOGY

I want us to take seriously how we prepare.

I want us to think hard about how we grow and protect our witness in the world.

In our current culture, it's easy to forget our mission.

Our mission is to make disciples of all nations. Our mission is to reflect the love of Christ.

Yet, in our current culture, culture wars are all around us. The question for people who truly desire to take their faith in Jesus seriously is not "Do we engage the culture around us?" But, "How do we engage culture around us?" It's not a matter of "if we do" but "as we do."

It's an Us vs. Them world out there.

Republican vs. Democrat.

PGA vs. LIV.

Jordan vs. LeBron.

Team Chris Rock vs. Team Will Smith.

As battle lines are drawn in culture wars, cancel culture has become the new fad. Over the past few years, there is nothing our culture won't cancel.

We'll cancel organizations, brands, restaurants, and people.

We'll cancel Nike because of their stance on Black Lives Matter.

We'll cancel an NBA all-star game because of legislation opposing gay marriage.

We'll cancel Starbucks because they refuse to say, "Merry Christmas."

We'll cancel Hobby Lobby because of convictions about healthcare and women's rights.

We'll cancel Chick-fil-a because of comments made about traditional marriage. (Though, let's be honest, people may cancel Chick-fil-a on social media on a Monday, but they're secretly ordering a #1 with a large sweat tea by Friday, right?)

We'll cancel the NFL and Hollywood.

COREOLOGY

We'll cancel pastors and churches.

We'll cancel the Disney Company because of their leftish agenda, but we will not cancel Disney World or Disneyland because, well, we have our priorities straight.

We'll cancel *cancel*.

As followers of Jesus, it doesn't take much for us to get off track and forget our mission. When we're off just a little, our core is distorted. We're not properly centered. One of the greatest challenges that cancel culture and culture wars present for us is that it is extremely difficult, if not impossible, to shine the light of Christ in places we have cancelled, neglected, or view as the enemy.

Presidential election years, as well as our current political climate, present constant distractions that ultimately mess with the core of who we are as followers of Jesus. When our core is off, our witness is off too.

As we journey through an election season, cancel culture, and culture wars, I want to be a voice that calls Jesus-followers to give serious attention to how we are protecting, developing, and cultivating our core.

I don't want us to confuse where our overall allegiance lies.

I don't want us to spend valuable energy fighting the wrong fights.

I don't want us to create enemies with people who are not enemies of God.

I don't want us to lose—or blow—our witness.

I don't want our hearts to become hard or our love to grow cold.

In his book *Though Shalt Not Be a Jerk*, Eugene Cho writes this, "When Christians—regardless of political leanings—behave like jerks and justify our behavior at all costs because of our ideological convictions, we bear false witness to Jesus Christ."[1]

---

[1] Eugene Cho, *Thou Shalt Not Be A Jerk*. (Colorado Spings, CO: David C Cook, 2020), 60.

COREOLOGY

I couldn't agree more. I have seen this happen all around me.

This book is not a plea to abandon conservative or progressive values. This book isn't a plea to vote for certain people or along party lines. This book isn't asking people to abandon the passion we have for certain issues.

This book is a plea to root our motives, intentions, passions, and desires in what it means to be Kingdom-people above all things. It is easier said than done.

Our core—the center of who we are—is the Kingship of Jesus Christ. If we neglect our core, we lose our center. We lose our balance. We hurt our witness.

Russell Moore says, "We now see young evangelicals walking away from evangelicalism not because they do not believe what the church teaches, but because they believe the church does not believe what the church teaches."[2]

---

[2] Russell Moore, "Why the Church Is Losing the Next Generation," Moore to

We know we can do better. And we know we can only do better when we are appropriately and properly rooted in what matters most.

Let's live with passion, yet be driven by principles that keep us properly rooted.

Passionate, yet driven by principles.

I want to offer six principles that function to keep us centered, rooted, and focused. They are simple, because they are meant to be remembered. They are specific yet broad enough to take on a life of their own in each person. The first three principles are focused on the inner-life, or as some may say, the vertical relationship we have with God. The last three principles are focused on the outer-life, the horizontal relationships we have with others.

1) I will daily confess that Jesus is the Lord of my life and nothing else is.

---

the Point, accessed November 29, 2021, http://createsend.com/t/r-6C1451630A966B6D2540EF23F30FeDED.

COREOLOGY

2) I will create and honor regular spiritual practices that remind me of my devotion to Jesus.

3) I will resist allowing any media outlet to become the primary way I think about culture and the world.

4) I will strive to become a peacemaker.

5) I will practice hospitality as a way to learn, grow, and invest in other people.

6) I will choose to regularly serve others.

As we drive on interstates and highways, we've all probably drifted just a little bit off track, and as we do, we've hit the highway strips. They're called sleeper lines, alert strips, highways strips, and rumble strips. Whatever you call them, these strips alert us that we're drifting off course. They aren't meant to make us panic. It doesn't mean we're completely off track or that we've made a wrong turn. It's a gentle signal to get back on track.

Think of this book as highway strips. Dozens of voices in our culture are fighting for our attention, affection, and allegiance. As Kingdom people, any form of drifting can lead to destruction.

Let's stay on track.

Jesus is worth it.

Chapter One

Principle #1: I will daily <u>confess</u> that Jesus is the Lord of my life and nothing else is.

What images come to mind when you think about making a confession?

Maybe you think about a courtroom when a hand is placed on a Bible and you're instructed, "Repeat after me, I swear to the tell the truth, the whole truth, and nothing but the truth, so help me God."

Maybe you think about a police officer taking a statement at the scene of an accident or crime.

Maybe you think about a confession booth.

Maybe you think about a moment in a worship experience when people get serious about sin.

COREOLOGY

Whatever image comes to mind, is it positive or negative? Is it hopeful? Or does it feel like punishment?

I think for most people connected to the Christian faith, when we think about confessing, we think about confessing sins.

The Bible speaks to this:

Matthew 3:5-6, "Then the people of Jerusalem and all Judea were going out to him, and all the region along the Jordan, and they were baptized by him in the river Jordan, **confessing** their sins."

1 John 1:9, "If we **confess** our sins, he is faithful and just and will forgive us our sins and purify us from all unrighteousness."

James 5:16, "Therefore **confess** your sins to each other and pray for each other so that you may be healed. The prayer of a righteous person is powerful and effective."

As Matthew, John, and James state, confessing sins is an important part of confession. However, it's worth

Principle 1: Confession

knowing that only four of the twenty-six times "confess" is used in the New Testament are referring to confessing sins. The other references are about swearing allegiance to Jesus and His Kingdom.

***

Although the Bible does refer to *confessing sins*, the primary way the Bible uses *confess* is allegiance to faith. It's not just how we confess our sins, but how we declare our faith. Amid dramatic election seasons and culture wars, how we practice confessing our faith is essential for our growth and development. Our witness to the world depends on it.

Let's talk about something we do every day of our lives: getting dressed. Hey, it's either talk about getting dressed or taking a few minutes to lead us all in a practice of confessing sins. Let's talk about getting dressed.

Are you ever confused or curious when you're attending a banquet and the dress attire is business casual? It's a term that still needs to be defined. We'll even text others we know attending the same event to ask what they're wearing. Are we thinking jeans

COREOLOGY

and a sports coat or suit without a tie? You probably don't want to be overly dressed for the occasion, but you also don't want to be the only person wearing khakis, an untucked shirt, and TOMS.

In the book of Ephesians, Paul ends his letter with a discussion on attire. This isn't for a banquet, wedding, funeral, dinner party, fundraising dinner, or a gala. What Paul has in mind is Kingdom-living, which involves engagement with the surrounding culture.

The ultimate issue at the end of Ephesians isn't if we engage the culture around us, but what we wear as we do. This isn't a suggestion. This is an expectation. This is a pretty big deal.

The city of Ephesus had major challenges to the Christian faith. It was a large, urban center. With close to 250,000 residents, it would be a large city by today's standards. It was home to over two dozen pagan temples, and with pagan temples often came temple prostitution. It was all about gratification and pleasure. Ephesus had the reputation for magic and witchcraft. Just read Acts 19 and consider the enormous impact such practices had on the city.

Principle 1: Confession

History tells us that there was a large keg fest held in the city each year. Nearly a million people descended upon Ephesus to engage in a first century form of Mardi Gras. This gives some context to Ephesians 5:19, "Don't get drunk on wine. Be filled with the Spirit." Ephesus natives would have known exactly what Paul was speaking into.

I'm not here to give you a complete historical analysis of first century Ephesus, but I do want to give you a sense of the immorality that existed in this city. Not only did Paul write a letter to the churches in Ephesus, but he also sent Timothy there to hunker down in order to establish a discipleship culture in the churches.

Not one time does Paul encourage the people to leave the city because of evil in the prevailing culture. He doesn't argue for a Christian colony, for cancel culture, or to run for your lives. He argues for witness, rooted identity, and for cultural engagement. And he does it by encouraging proper dress attire.

His benediction begins with one word, "Finally!" After all he has written on identity, the power of God, reconciliation, household codes, and how leaders are

COREOLOGY

to equip the church for works of service, he now prepares people for engagement, not isolation.

"Finally," Paul writes in Ephesians 6:10-11, "Be strong in the Lord and in his mighty power. Put on the full armor of God, so that you can take your stand against the devil's schemes."

Put on the full armor. It's a phrase he's going to come back to in a couple of sentences, but not before providing clarity on the enemy we are up against, "For our struggle is not against flesh and blood, but against the rulers, against the authorities, against the powers of this dark world and against the spiritual forces of evil in the heavenly realms."

In a culture full of enemies of righteousness, godliness, and character, Paul wants people to know that humans are to be engaged for God, not predetermined enemies.

He comes back to the rally cry in 6:13, "Put on the full armor of God."

The fight he's preparing people for is for the sake of the mission of God. It is *for* something. Not to protect

Principle 1: Confession

something. It is not for the preservation of the Roman Empire, a nation, or even for the eternal Kingdom of God. In a city full of theaters, halls for every form of philosophy, and pagan temples, Paul paints a picture of how we engage culture without getting lost in culture wars. His message wasn't to protest keg fests and to cancel marketplaces and to boycott parts of town, but to dress yourself as people of the Kingdom and to live in a way that you make a difference in the world.

In 1 Timothy, Paul is writing to Timothy as a leader in the Ephesian churches. When it came to Paul's advice on how Timothy should choose and commission elders of the churches in the city, one character trait needed was, "He must also have a good reputation with outsiders." This was a needed trait in order to pastor a church and engage a culture.

Paul is preparing Jesus-followers for cultural engagement by giving them a visual image of what it means to be dressed for engagement.

COREOLOGY

I'll paraphrase Paul's charge to dress for engagement:

- Fasten the belt of truth.
- Put on the breastplate of righteousness.
- Feet fitted with the gospel of peace.
- Take up the shield of faith.
- Take the helmet of salvation.
- Take the sword of the Spirit.

No soldier would get dressed for battle and leave behind a vital piece of armor. Being partially dressed isn't going to help you in combat.

Paul doesn't unpack an image and suggest that 80% of the armor is good enough. Nope. What matters is that people are fully armored up for the task ahead.

The issue driving Paul isn't whether Christians (and the local church) choose to engage the culture around them, it is what they are supposed to wear as they do.

***

This is why cancel culture isn't good for the church. It is why getting lost in culture wars doesn't advance the Kingdom of God. And it is why when we get lost in

Principle 1: Confession

election seasons by choosing sides, creating enemies who aren't enemies of God, and giving into fear tactics, it greatly hinders the motivation and determination to passionately engage people. It is difficult to win to Christ those our media outlets call opponents.

This brings me back to the idea of confession. To confess Jesus as the Lord of one's life has always been to swear ultimate allegiance to Him, not to any earthly king, kingdom, or kingdom agenda. To confess that Jesus is the Lord of your life is to also declare that no one else, and nothing else, is. This kind of confession is meant to change everything.

Your confession becomes your lifestyle. It is your heartbeat. Your motivation. Your legacy. It is everything.

In order not to lose our Christian witness, it's essential that we embody this principle: *I will daily confess that Jesus is the Lord of my life and nothing else is*.

When I hear Christians say, "The gospel is about individual freedom, rights, and choices," you know what I think? I think this is probably a person who has

COREOLOGY

been influenced by progressive politics, not someone who is immersing themselves in the life and teachings of Jesus found in Matthew, Mark, Luke, and John.

When I hear Christians say, "Christians needs to stand for Biblical values," and the next thing out of their mouths is a statement about abortion or homosexuality, you know what I think? I think this is probably a person who has been influenced by conservative politics, not someone who is immersing themselves in the life and teachings of Jesus found in Matthew, Mark, Luke, and John.

Too harsh?

My point is that sometimes it seems the way we talk reflects our politics and/or ideologies, more than our Savior and King. It's hard to engage a culture if we have given into the culture.

Take this to heart—if there are culture wars that we are passionate about, and it seems like there is a loss (maybe because of an election, a vote, or legislation), the Kingdom of God can still advance in the world. Therefore, we don't lose. We, as followers of Jesus, keep moving with God.

Principle 1: Confession

It is possible to confess Jesus with our lips, yet give our allegiance to the kingdoms of this world.

It is possible to confess Jesus as Savior, yet never confess Him as Lord.

***

Paul writes Ephesians to awaken the people to their new identity as cross-shaped, empty-tomb-living, Jesus-confessing people. Our confession of faith becomes a daily reminder of the life we now live in God. If the church fails to remind each other what our mission is in the world, and if we fail to repeat it, we will slowly forget it. And when we forget it, we will replace it with other missions in the world. And when we replace it, we may just try to wrap it in Christian language in order to sound Christian-y. If we aren't careful, we let our social, political, and cultural issues inform how we think about Jesus, instead of letting Jesus inform how we think about all issues in the world.

Our confession prepares us for engagement. What kind of battle are we preparing ourselves for? Who is our enemy? What are we equipping ourselves for?

COREOLOGY

***

Andy Stanley, in his book *Not In It to Win It*, says this, "All Democrats are not morally corrupt, anti-God, anti-family, and anti-church, and all Republicans are not anti-voting-rights, anti-healthcare, and anti-vaccine. Let's not participate in that type of labeling. This kind of rhetoric divides American from American. It divides Christian from Christian as well."[3]
I couldn't agree more.

2020 was one of the hardest years of many of our lives. For many of my pastor-friends, it was one of the most difficult years of ministry. We had a heated presidential election season, COVID, and social unrest. And to make it worse, we were left attempting to communicate messages of hope, grief, joy, and loss all while looking at screens. The year 2020 didn't create division and animosity, it brought it to light. It revealed how much we love to win! And as Americans, it revealed how much we also hate to lose!
Again, Andy Stanley writes, "And what does the evangelical church in America value most? Winning.

---

[3] Andy Stanley, *Not In It to Win It*. (Grand Rapids, MI: Zondervan, 2022), 51.

Principle 1: Confession

What do we fear? Losing . . . the problem I'm referring to—the Achilles' heel in modern evangelicalism—is our obsession with winning."[4]

We want to win. We do not want to lose. And we especially do not want to lose to *them* (whoever the *them* is).

For any of you sport fans, you have the teams you cheer for, but you also know the teams you love to see lose.

In my life, I don't mind losing a game of cards to my friend Amy, I just don't want to lose to Brad. I don't mind losing fantasy football to Jimmy, I just don't want to lose to Todd.

When we get wrapped up in culture wars and in the heat of election seasons, the core of who we are will be challenged. Remember, it doesn't take much to move us away from the center.

---

[4] Ibid, xxi.

COREOLOGY

In his book, *Justice in the Bible*, Tim Keller writes, "When the church as a whole is no longer seen as speaking to questions that transcend politics, and when it is no longer united by a common faith that transcends politics, then the world sees strong evidence that Nietzsche, Freud, and Marx were right, that religion is really just a cover for people wanting to get their way in the world."[5]

Hopefully, we read that and desire to do better.

***

Conversion has always been a vital part of the Christian story. Conversion means to change, alter, and to make something different. It is not to add to what I already have. We are converted *from* and *into*. In his book *Jesus for President*, Shane Claiborne says it like this, "We need conversion in the best sense of the word—people who are marked by the renewing of their minds and imaginations, who no longer conform to the pattern that is destroying our world. Otherwise we have only believers, not converts."

---

[5] Timothy Keller, "Justice in the Bible," Life in the Gospel, accessed November 29, 2001, https://quarterly.gospelinlife.com/justice-in-the-bible/.

Principle 1: Confession

As vital as conversion is to the Christian faith, confession is vital to conversion.

Our confession is meant to center us, transform us, and redirect us. Confession sets us on a trajectory to live with one ultimate allegiance, not dozens of them. Jesus is Lord, nothing else is.

Our conversion sets us on a life of following Jesus, and our confession keeps us on track.

Listen to a few of the voices in the Bible as they speak about the power of confession:

John 12:42, "Nevertheless many, even of the authorities, believed in him. But because of the Pharisees they did not **confess** it, for fear that they would be put out of the synagogue."

Romans 10:9-10, "If you **confess** with your lips that Jesus is Lord and believe in your heart that God raised him from the dead, you will be saved. For one believes with the heart and so is justified, and one **confesses** with the mouth and so is saved."

COREOLOGY

2 Corinthians 9:13, "Through the testing of this ministry you glorify God by your obedience to the **confession** of the gospel of Christ and by the generosity of your sharing with them and with all others."

Philippians 2:9-11, "Therefore God also highly exalted him and gave him the name that is above every name, so that at the name of Jesus every knee should bend, in heaven and on earth and under the earth, and every tongue should **confess** that Jesus Christ is Lord, to the glory of God the Father."

1 Timothy 6:12, "Fight the good fight of the faith; take hold of the eternal life, to which you were called and for which you made the good **confession** in the presence of many witnesses."

Hebrews 3:1, "Therefore, brothers and sisters, holy partners in a heavenly calling, consider that Jesus, the apostle and high priest of our **confession**."

Hebrews 4:14, "Since, then, we have a great high priest who has passed through the heavens, Jesus, the Son of God, let us hold fast to our **confession**."

Principle 1: Confession

Confession isn't a once-in-lifetime spiritual expression. It is a daily practice that centers us in the heart of God. Develop a practice every day of swearing allegiance to the one and only King who is eternal. In your practice, remind yourself that Jesus is Lord, and no one else is.

Dress yourself for engagement.

Don't shrink back in fear.

Press forward in faith.

Remember that a confession is not just to be believed, but lived.

Chapter Two

Principle #2: I will create and honor regular spiritual practices that remind me of my <u>devotion</u> to Jesus.

Most of us are familiar with C.S. Lewis's work as an author, storyteller, and thought-provoker. His personal secretary, Walter Hooper, once described Lewis as the most converted man he had ever met. Of course, he was far from perfection, yet so much of his life had become inhabited by Christ. Wouldn't we all love to leave a similar legacy where someone might stand up at our funeral and say, "Here's one thing I definitely know about this person, they were without a shadow of a doubt a converted child of God."

COREOLOGY

Wouldn't you love for people to say something similar about you?

Conversion is a life-long journey. Said differently, the Christian life is not about status change alone. It's not just going from unsaved to saved or lost to found. The language Peter chooses in his first letter is that we get to "grow into our salvation."[6]

Spiritual growth is about responding to the invitation of God, far more than being pushed by God. Think about the difference between being invited and pushed. Think about the difference between how a shepherd leads sheep and how cattleman drive livestock. Through grace, God invites us into deeper places. Though we will never arrive as fully converted people, God will never cease to invite us to go deeper, to grow closer, and to surrender just a little bit more.

Jesus said this in Matthew 6:33, "But seek first the Kingdom of God and His righteousness, and all these things will be given to you as well." In the Greek, the word "seek" is zeteite. It means to look for in order to

---

[6] 1 Peter 2:2.

Principle 2: Devotion

find, or to devote serious effort to realize one's desire or objective. It's not just a matter of believing the right things, but that our heart is cultivated in a way that we pursue and seek. The language Jesus chose to use in this moment wasn't to "seek His face" or to "seek His truth" or to "seek His heart." It was to "seek His Kingdom."

***

It's interesting that when it comes to physical and mental health, we put together plans. We develop diet plans, workout plans, and possibly put in place forms of accountability. We know that physical and mental health takes intentionality, focus, and forms of structure. However, when it comes to spiritual growth, many Christians think that it will happen over time. We think that if we show up to church, pray before meals, and don't visit night clubs then maybe, somehow, spiritual growth will just happen.

When it comes to responding to Jesus' words about seeking after God's Kingdom and righteousness, the question isn't do you, but how do you? How is it that you seek after the Kingdom of God?

COREOLOGY

***

In order to guard our hearts from getting lost in culture wars, and even election seasons, it is imperative that we commit to the following: ***I will create and honor regular spiritual practices that remind me of my devotion to Jesus.***

You can't give God a 3-minute devotional time in the morning, yet soak in cable news and podcasts for hours a day and think you can live a life devoted to Christ. I'm not arguing that we live like hermits and carve out hours upon hours of time every day for prayer and Bible study. I am arguing that devotion to Jesus takes practices that keep us rooted, grounded, and growing. Without such practices, we will drift from the center. We will fail to strengthen our core.

Maybe you are reading this book and you care nothing about politics and you attempt to avoid cultural issues when at all possible. I hope that I encourage you that your witness for Christ means something to the culture around us. How you engage in spiritual practices will keep you grounded.

Principle 2: Devotion

Maybe you are reading this book and you fully identify with a political party. It's the card you carry. I hope that I can encourage you to live life with convictions, be passionate about the world around you, but work hard not to confuse the Kingdom of God with party affiliation.

The Great Commission calls us to, "Go into the world and make disciples."[7] It isn't, "Wait inside your church or house and see if people will just come to you." We are sent out.

What we are finding in the current cultural climate is that it's draining to engage with people who think and vote differently. When culture is toxic it's not life-giving or joyful.

Most people credit a sociologist from the University of Virginia as the one who coined the term *culture wars*. In the late 1980s and early 1990s, James Davison Hunter was conducting research concerning how people engage cultural issues. The phrase "if feels like war" kept popping up.

---

[7] Matthew 28:18-20.

COREOLOGY

From President Raegan's "war of drugs" to Focus on the Family's "war on the family," language of "war" became the term to describe cultural engagement. A few decades later, it's the language that still permeates. It has wounded us. We still haven't recovered.

Listen to the rhetoric of many church-going, Bible-believing Christians around us today. It's language of defeat. It's hard to live from a place of victory in Christ when you give into a message of division, disconnection, and polarization. Living from a place of victory takes practice, commitment, and focus. Jesus deserves it.

Back to Matthew 6:33. In fact, look at the entire narrative found in 6:25-33. Listen for words like "worry," "is not life more," and "are you not much more." Pay attention to the content that leads up to Jesus's words about seeking His Kingdom.

25 "Therefore I tell you, do not worry about your life, what you will eat or drink; or about your body, what you will wear. Is not life more than food, and the body more than clothes? 26 Look at the birds of the air; they do not sow or reap or store away in barns, and yet

Principle 2: Devotion

your heavenly Father feeds them. Are you not much more valuable than they? ²⁷ Can any one of you by worrying add a single hour to your life?

²⁸ "And why do you worry about clothes? See how the flowers of the field grow. They do not labor or spin. ²⁹ Yet I tell you that not even Solomon in all his splendor was dressed like one of these. ³⁰ If that is how God clothes the grass of the field, which is here today and tomorrow is thrown into the fire, will he not much more clothe you—you of little faith? ³¹ So do not worry, saying, 'What shall we eat?' or 'What shall we drink?' or 'What shall we wear?' ³² For the pagans run after all these things, and your heavenly Father knows that you need them.³³ But seek first his kingdom and his righteousness, and all these things will be given to you as well.

No one else in first century culture talked like this or taught this. No one was teaching things like how seeking a kingdom could bring stability, peace, reduction of worry, and provision. Authoritative voices in those times most likely taught about kingdom in a way that induced worry and fear, not reduced.

COREOLOGY

And remember, Jesus offers this teaching in the middle of what is known as the Sermon on the Mount. It's a sermon that begins with the word "blessed." Before Jesus began speaking these words, He graciously cured the sick, those with various diseases, the demon-possessed, and those tormented by distress. The crowd of listeners had just experienced incredible mercy. They had also experienced years of worry, fear, and marginalization. Jesus drew them near, cured their physical diseases, gave them community, and spoke to them about a Kingdom that was worth seeking because of the blessings it brings, not the fear it induces.

***

The Chapman University Survey of American Fears (CSAF) is an ongoing project to gauge what Americans are afraid of. Each year, they attempt to discover what it is that strikes fear in us. They have been tracking data and doing research for a decade, and once a year, they release their list. They want to know what terrifies Americans and causes us to worry.

Principle 2: Devotion

In 2023, their list went like this:

10—Biological warfare.
9—Pollution of oceans, rivers, and lakes.
8—Economic/financial collapse.
7—Not having enough money for the future.
6—Pollution of drinking water.
5—The United States becoming involved in another world war.
4—People I love dying.
3—Russia using nuclear weapons.
2—People I love becoming seriously ill.
1—Corrupt government officials.[8]

It's important to note that this research was released before another war broke out in the middle east. I'm not sure if much on this list surprises you. It does go to show that we live in a nation with a lot of worry and fear, and let's be honest, some of it is for good reason.

A lot of the fear, worry, and anger people experience in our world today is induced by cable news, social

---

[8] https://www.chapman.edu/wilkinson/research-centers/babbie-center/_files/2023%20Fear/23csaf-9-top-10-list-2023.pdf.

COREOLOGY

media, and the way certain networks and journalists tell the stories about events around us. I heard someone say one time that the political left is driven by anger and the political right is driven by fear. That's not totally accurate, but it's also not too far off base. Now, with that said, there are reasons to be angry, and there are reasons to be afraid.

Watch Fox News for a few minutes and you get a pretty large dose of fearmongering. Switch over to CNN or MSNBC and the way stories are told is meant to foster a strong emotional reaction. When people come to me who are struggling with deep forms of worry and fear about the world around us—the kind of fear and worry that is both paralyzing and keeps us from loving our neighbors—I know that there is a very good chance that this is someone who takes in large doses of the news every day. Striking fear in people both protects and increases ratings and clicks. However, it never advances the good of the Kingdom of God. In fact, it sets up barriers and walls that oppose the very Kingdom Jesus inaugurated.

When Jesus says, "Seek first the Kingdom of God and His righteousness," Jesus is asking for allegiance, trust, and utter dependence in His Kingdom.

Principle 2: Devotion

The word "kingdom" is used about one-hundred sixty-two times in the New Testament. Matthew uses it fifty-three times in his Gospel. Jesus said things like, "My Kingdom is not of this world. If it were, my servants would fight to prevent my arrest by the Jews. But now my Kingdom is from another place,"[9] and, "The Kingdom of God does not come with your careful observations, nor will people say, 'Here it is,' or 'There it is,' because the Kingdom of God is within you."[10]

When teaching his disciples to pray, Jesus added, "Your Kingdom come, your will be done, on earth as it is in heaven."[11]

It would have been helpful if Jesus would have taken the time to define the Kingdom of God. It was obvious that how He thought about the Kingdom was utterly different than how everyone else around him was taught to think about kingdom. Yet, he never clearly

---

[9] John 18:36.

[10] Luke 27:20-21.

[11] Matthew 6:10.

COREOLOGY

stated, "The Kingdom of God is..." Instead, his phrase was, "The Kingdom of God is like..."

In describing the Kingdom of God, Jesus chose to tell stories. Lots of them. He didn't give a definition that could fit into a Webster dictionary. He chose to use stories more than definitions, because He deeply cared about His people imagining a new world transformed by all the values He ushered into the world. This Kingdom wasn't about control, manipulation, and unhealthy power, but about invitation, opportunity, and Divine-connection.

Marcus Borg writes, "In His world, 'Kingdom' language was political. Jesus' hearers knew about other kingdoms—the kingdom of Herod and the kingdom of Rome. The kingdom of God had to be something different from those kingdoms. The Kingdom of God is for the earth. The Lord's Prayer speaks of God's kingdom coming on earth, even as it already exists in heaven. It is about the transformation of this world—what life would be on earth if God were ruler and the lords of the domination systems were not."[12]

---

[12] Marcus J. Borg, "Jesus and Politics," Bible Odyssey, accessed October 9, 2019, https://fr.bibleodyssey.com/articles/jesus-and-politics/.

Principle 2: Devotion

I want to make this clear, loyalty to the Kingdom of God doesn't mean we don't care about earthly kingdoms. You will never hear me say that issues don't matter, or policies don't matter, or government doesn't matter, or that voting doesn't matter. However, I will always push against forms of nationalism that confuse the eternal Kingdom with an earthly kingdom. And if you are a follower of Jesus, you should too. There is no country on earth—including the country I love and call home—that is more loved or cherished by God than any other. We serve a global God who means it when He says, "For God so loved the world."[13]

One of my favorite authors, Philip Yancey, writes, "I worry about the recent surge of power among U.S. Christians, who seem to be focusing more and more on political means. Once Christians were ignored or scorned; now they are courted by every savvy politician."[14]

---

[13] John 3:16.

[14] Philip Yancey, *The Jesus I Never Knew*. (Grand Rapids, MI: Zondervan, 1995), 246.

COREOLOGY

And he wrote this in his book *The Jesus I Never Knew*, in 1995!

A few paragraphs later, Yancey writes, "Passing laws to enforce morality serves a necessary function, to dam up evil, but it never solves human problems. If a century from now all that historians can say about evangelicals of the 1990s is that they stood for family values, then we will have failed the mission Jesus gave us to accomplish: to communicate God's reconciling love to *sinners*."[15]

Jesus intended for His followers to live by a different set of rules than any earthly kingdom sets in place. And He still does. Our King is in place. His Kingdom has been set in motion. Through Jesus's death, burial, and resurrection, we have citizenship in this Kingdom. We have values, principles, and commands. We have a mission to build bridges in order to invite others in instead of building walls to keep others out. This is what the church—Jesus's church—has been tasked to pray for and to live into.

---

[15] Philip Yancey, *The Jesus I Never Knew*. (Grand Rapids, MI: Zondervan, 1995), 247.

Principle 2: Devotion

Again, Yancey writes, "If the gates of hell cannot prevail against the church, the contemporary political scene hardly offers much threat."[16]

***

Devotion to Jesus is a spiritual practice. It is so much more than a one-time experience through confession, repentance, and baptism. This kind of devotion invites growth and transformation. It needs structure, intentionality, and focus.

Let me encourage you, especially in election seasons, double down on spiritual practices and the time and energy you give to Jesus. There are eighty-nine chapters in the four Gospels. This means that you can read all four Gospels in one month by reading three chapters a day. If that is too much for you, read one chapter a day, and you can read through all four in one quarter.

Especially in passionate seasons when our allegiance is tested (like in election years), spiritual practices are

---

[16] Philip Yancey, *The Jesus I Never Knew.* (Grand Rapids, MI: Zondervan, 1995), 250.

COREOLOGY

critical not just for our growth, but to keep us centered. Our core needs daily attention. Consider developing a Rule of Life this year. It's a commitment to specific spiritual practices.[17] Discipleship needs discipline.

God isn't interested in you developing practices only for the sake of checking boxes. God is interested in practices that fill you with joy because of how they keep you connected to Jesus and to people. God knows the fruit that comes from a disciplined life.

There is no worldly kingdom that can provide the peace, nurturing, and care that we need. It can't. Every earthly kingdom has a lifespan. Either they will fail, or one day when Jesus returns, they will be remembered no more. Yet, the Kingdom of God will go on forever. In this Kingdom, we never have to guess or wonder who the King is. There is no four-year term or bid for reelection. He isn't interested in campaigning for attention, affection, or donations. There will be no commercials attempting to demonize

---

[17] The appendix has a few *Rule of Life* resources that are meant to help encourage you as you consider your own.

Principle 2: Devotion

His opponents. His movement is ongoing and everlasting.

As Christians, we can't have an eternal Kingdom without surrendering to the one and only King.

Daily surrendering.

Daily practicing.

Daily committing to grow in Christ.

Chapter 3

Principle #3: I will <u>resist</u> allowing any media outlet to become the primary way I think about culture and the world.

In some parts of life, a verbal yes or no is required.

If you have ever been on a flight, you've had to endure the boarding process. Though passengers are asked to not clog up the boarding lanes until their boarding number is called, we all know how this works. The moment concierge and Group 1 are called, Group 9 rushes to the front of the line as if Ikea just opened their doors on Black Friday. It's a mad rush. Now, if you're sitting on an exit row next to an emergency exit, when you scan your ticket, you will be asked if you are willing to help in the case of an emergency.

COREOLOGY

This is not a trick question. To move forward in the boarding
process, you must give a verbal "yes." It can't be a shrug, head nod, or a thumbs up. You have to speak the word, "Yes."

I have had the honor to perform numerous weddings in my ministry career. When we get to the part in the wedding ceremony in which I ask if they take each other as their spouse, I've never had a groom or bride respond with, "I guess so" or "I think so" or "we've made it this far, so, why not?" Even if someone said something like this in jest, I think I would either repeat the question or reframe the seriousness of the moment. A verbal "yes" is required.

***

In Christianity, a yes is essential when it comes to following Jesus. In fact, God's yes to us is what got this whole thing started in the first place. And as we are invited into this life with Jesus, we are asked to give our yes to Him. This is a part of why I felt compelled to write this book. Our confession matters more than we think it does. It sealed a covenant between Jesus and us. Yet, our yeses are meant to be so much more than

Principle 3: Resistance

a verbal commitment; they're meant to be a commitment we choose to respond to for the rest of our lives.

Let's be clear, the "yes" we speak in our conversion isn't a yes to heaven, or a yes to baptism, or a yes to the church. It's a yes to Jesus. Our yes is to a person who died for the sins of the world and rose again to give us new life. Our yes is to the journey with Jesus, not just a destination with Him after we die.

As we attempt to live out our confession, we also need to take the noes we speak seriously as well. I think we all get the importance of the yes. I think everything you have read so far in this chapter you'd agree with. However, speaking a "no" probably brings more questions. What are we saying "no" to? Who are we saying "no" to? I'm glad you asked.

***

Ancient baptism practices in some parts of the world include a yes and a no. What you say no to—or what you renounce—is preparation for the yes to Christ. Think about the power of this in anyone's conversion story. It's as if people are invited to say, "As I live into

COREOLOGY

my relationship with Christ, there are some things I need to say no to right now because they can't go with me into my new life. I must leave them behind. I must renounce them."

Dating back to ancient Israel, Sabbath-keeping was a regular rhythm in the lives of God's people. It was a way to say no to work, production, and control, which provided the necessary space for people to be reminded of God's power, existence, providence, and care. While most of the 10 commandments are stated in one sentence, the command about the Sabbath gets an entire paragraph. Maybe God knew our addiction and love for work, busyness, and production, that He knew this one needed elaboration. To honor and practice Sabbath, a "no" was required.

In the Bible, fasting is mentioned over seventy times. In the Sermon on the Mount, Jesus speaks on three spiritual practices, and each one begins with this statement, "When you . . ."[18] Jesus's words on giving, praying, and fasting are stated as if Jesus assumes

---

[18] Matthew 6:2, 7, and 16.

Principle 3: Resistance

they will be done. In the context of Matthew 6, it's as if an assumption carries more weight than a command.

Now, when it comes to how the Bible speaks about fasting, food is always involved. Always. There are different types of fasts found in the Bible, but each one involves saying no to food in some way. This is difficult for most of us, because we don't just eat breakfast, lunch, and dinner, but snacks in between. The idea of skipping meals sends some of us into depression just thinking about it. Food is life. And for the love of all that is good, please don't ask me to give up chips and salsa.

Yet, in the Bible, saying "no" to food on a semi-regular basis was to serve as a reminder of how God so graciously provides for us.

***

Friends, I feel like I have taken way too much time to lead up to this point about resistance, but I think we needed some context to get there. When it comes to how frequently we take in social media, cable news, and any content about events happening in the world, if we don't have parameters, boundaries, and

COREOLOGY

practices, we set ourselves up to have a tainted view of the world around us. Though fasting in the Bible always involved food, in our culture today there are principles that need to be applied to any form of consumption. Our hearts were not created by God to take in large doses of media every day. As Christians, we need to practice noes, resistance, and restraint when it comes to how we engage content about current events. Remember, we must learn to engage culture. But as we do, we must do this as people who are passionate and intentional about protecting our hearts from any narrative that attempts to harden them.

Let's face it, those of us living in the United States of America live in a binary system. For many people, you are either democrat or republican, conservative or liberal. Those are the options. When I first moved to Memphis, people just assumed I was a Republican. I was white, from the south, a pastor connected to the evangelical stream of Christianity, and at the time we lived in the suburbs. Not to stereotype, but it was a fairly safe assumption.

However, I'm not a Republican. I'm also not a Democrat. I've never aligned with a political party or

Principle 3: Resistance

platform. At one time in my life I claimed to be apolitical, but too many people heard that as wishy-washy. I do care about politics because I care about the world. I have voted across the lines many times since the first time I was able to vote in 2000. Yet, some were shocked when I didn't fit within their conservative box. And here's the deal, if you only believe in a binary system, what often happens is this: "If you're not in my box, there's only one other box to put you in."

"If you're not in my conservative camp, you're one of *them*."

"If you're not in my progressive camp, you're one of *them*."

This is just how the game is played.

Most news outlets work hard to generate allegiances and alliances, and one of the most effective ways to do this is to play by the rules of a binary system. It has proven to work. And when we give in to this kind of system, it makes unity, fellowship, and even evangelism extremely difficult.

COREOLOGY

What if we choose to refuse to give into this logic by intentionally limiting our consumption of media? What if we attempt to fast from cable news, iPhone apps, or social media for the sake of our sanity? I'm not suggesting that we give it up all together. But what if we diligently choose to not give in to the us vs. them rhetoric?

In his book *Resilient*, John Eldridge describes a friend who took in heavy doses of media each day. This friend was stressed, depressed, and often in a rage. He chose to significantly limit the amount of media he took in each day. The fruit of resisting led him to say, "I have more peace and joy in my life now than I ever have."[19] And you know who else also felt the change in a positive way? His wife!

I want to challenge our media consumption in three ways. Hopefully at least one of these will resonate with you.

***

---

[19] John Eldridge, *Resilient*. (Nashville, TN: Thomas Nelson, 2022), 36.

Principle 3: Resistance

One, fear is used as a weapon to motivate.

As I wrote in an earlier chapter, I've heard friends say that the political left is driven by anger and the political right by fear. Fear is profitable. Fear is fuel. Fear motivates. Fear gets people to buy in to forms of security. Fear unites people around a cause. Fear creates common enemies. Fear isolates. Fear creates unnecessary forms of anxiety. Fear strangles joy. Fear does not bring about hope in God or hope for the world. Fear does not bring about a deeper love for God, for God's mission, or for the world.

Research shows that fear-based messaging is nearly twice as effective as messaging that fails to stir that particular emotion. A lot of times, what we hear is something like this:

The other party is out to destroy you.

You know they hate America, right?

They are all racists.

They are all socialists.

COREOLOGY

They want to open up all the borders.

They want to kill everybody at the border.

Someone once said that dwelling on fear and outrage is spiritually deforming.

I'd take it a step further. Giving into fear slowly rots the soul. Giving into fear slowly destroys every path for evangelism. It does not bring about the peace, unity, and justice of God.

Fear rarely generates positive responses. It produces far more negativity than positivity.

Negative thoughts lower your state of mind. They separate and divide.

If there is anything in our lives igniting the emotion of fear, it must be dealt with by pushing back against the source that drives the emotion.

***

Two, the truth about what is going in our culture and world is hard to find.

Principle 3: Resistance

We've never had easier access to the news than we do today. Yet, where do we go to be informed about the news without being dealt heavy doses of biases? And if you truly think that your news outlet is bias free, this point is for you.

In his book *Thou Shalt Not Be a Jerk* by Eugene Cho, he refers to a story from 2012 that most of us probably remember. In 2012, Mitt Romney was challenging Barack Obama's reelection bid for presidency. Tension was mounting. As we've come to find in every election season, commercials and advertisements are not just about what a candidate has to offer, but how dreadfully awful the opposing candidate is as a person and leader.

An image quickly went viral on the internet. Romney was pictured having his shoes shined before boarding a private plane to head to his next event. On the internet, people went nuts. However, as the image went viral, it wasn't just the one image of Romney having his shoes shined that swept the internet. It was placed next to an image of President Obama fist bumping a janitor. Is the internet not crafty, or what? The messaging behind the images people saw on twitter, Facebook, and Instagram was simple, one

COREOLOGY

candidate lives a privileged life. The other candidate is here for the people.

Now, let me say this about former President Obama. There is little doubt in my mind that he would fist bump janitors, and not just when the cameras were rolling. However, the image of Mitt Romney having his shoes shined was not what it seemed. It's what the internet wanted people to believe. Actually, Romney was sitting in a chair as a TSA agent performed security measures to ensure that passengers were safe to fly on a plane.

David Rand is a MIT cognitive scientist. In his book *Thou Shalt Not Be a Jerk*, Eugene Cho references research that Rand performed gauging how people take in fake news. What he found is that on average, people are inclined to believe false news at least 20% of the time. Here's what Rand wrote, "But when we resist snap judgments, we are harder to fool. You just have to stop and think, all of the data we have collected suggest that's the real problem. It's not that people are being super-biased and using their reasoning ability to trick themselves into believing crazy stuff. It's just that people aren't stopping. They're rolling on."[20]

Principle 3: Resistance

People will repost, share, and pass along information without even clicking on the link.

We give credence to what we want to believe is true, not on what is actually true.

A lot of times, we pay more attention to what people have to say about current events than we do about the current event.

This isn't just true in politics.

When we celebrated our first anniversary, Kayci surprised me with Dish Network. This was 2003. For our first year of marriage, we didn't have cable. We had an antenna and dial-up internet. With Dish Network, I now had ESPN after living a year without it. As a sports fanatic, I deserved a trophy, right?

In 2003, ESPN began shifting their content and production from what it was back in the 1990s. Fox

---

[20] Steinmetz, "How Your Brain," http://time.com/5362183/the-real-fake-news-crisis/.

COREOLOGY

Sports had come along and created a rivalry. To get a competitive advantage, ESPN launched new shows like Pardon the Interruption and Around the Horn. Two decades later, I still watch these shows. However, they drive Kayci nuts. Basically, they are shows where people yell, scream, and argue their points about what is happening in the world of sports. It's not just that they cover the story, they cover what they think about the story. There's a difference.

In sports, politics, and even religion, it's often the loudest and angriest who win the day. Whether it's PTI or Glenn Beck, it's the spin on the story that boosts ratings, not the story itself. For many news outlets, it's not just how you win the argument, but how you crush, shame, and destroy the opponent in the process of trying to win the argument.

Jesus plays by a different set of rules. For Jesus, it isn't that the loudest and angriest win the day, but that the most truthful and grace-filled win the day.

We live in a time where anyone with a smartphone can become a journalist. Yet, if we really believe that Jesus is the way, the truth, and the life, then we must

Principle 3: Resistance

allow Him to be the narrative that shapes every other narrative.

***

Thirdly, projection impacts engagement.

When we project upon people a certain stereotype or ideology, we hinder our willingness and desire to meet people where they are.

When you're driving down the road and you see someone with a Trump or Biden bumper sticker, what do you think? What's going through your head? If you pull into the same restaurant, are you likely to speak to the person? Or have you already decided what it is you think about them?

This is true in a lot of areas of life. When you see someone with a hoodie representing a certain sports team, you determine ahead of time how you will interact with them. If it's an Alabama fan, they are probably conceited and narcissistic. If you see someone in a Dallas Cowboy jersey, they are most likely compassionate and humble. And you see, I have just created a couple of scenarios that prove my point.

COREOLOGY

We project.

How we project impacts engagement.

For Jesus-followers, our beginning place must be that all people have been created in the image of God and are worthy of redemption and community. No matter what bumper stickers or t-shirts may say, people are redeemable. They are not our enemies. Therefore, we approach them as image-bearers of God, not as enemies of the cross. We don't allow other humans to generate narratives for us. Jesus is the ultimate narrative.

***

Devotion to Christ needs a daily yes and a daily no.

Yes to Christ and no to the many voices of the world.

We say yes to Jesus and no to other voices so that we can say yes to people.

Occasionally—maybe often—delete the app.
Stay away from cable news.

Principle 3: Resistance

Resist the urge to only converse with people who look like you, vote like you, smell like you, and live like you.

The world—your world—will be a more peaceful place.

Chapter 4

Principle #4: I will strive to become a *peacemaker*.

I enjoy working jigsaw puzzles. I need a hobby that forces me to slow down and practice patience. Puzzles do just that. My friend Josh Graves's wife, Kara, enjoys working puzzles too. Yet, it drives Josh crazy the way she goes about it. When you work a thousand-piece puzzle it's going to take a few days. You spread the pieces out over a dining room table, and you go to work. For Graves, it's not that you can't use the dining room table for a few days or weeks. What frustrates him is what happens when Kara finishes the puzzle. She inserts the final piece, takes a few looks at the puzzle, nods her head in approval, and then crumbles it up and puts the pieces back in the cardboard box. Graves, maybe because he is an enneagram three,

COREOLOGY

thinks the completion of a puzzle deserves a little bit more celebratory activity. Why not invite some friends over to see the final product? At least take a few pictures and post the accomplishment online, right? Gloat a little bit! Don't just put the puzzle up.

Working a puzzle takes time. When you begin, you must know it's a process. There's a very good chance you will not complete the project in one sitting.

It takes patience. If you are lacking in patience, don't begin the journey of piecing a puzzle together.

It takes strategy. You need to organize pieces by color, design, or shape.

It takes effort and perseverance. Unless you want to occupy a table for months at a time, you need to keep coming back to the puzzle until it is completed.

The same is true for almost anything we attempt to make or build in life. Whether it is a large Lego set or working in a woodshop creating cutting boards or pens, making something takes time, patience, strategy, and effort. You must be committed to the process if you care to reap the benefits of the results.

Principle 4: Peacemaking

***

In Matthew 5, Jesus begins the Sermon on the Mount with what we call the Beatitudes. The Beatitudes are statements that begin with the word "Blessed." Jesus begins this famous sermon by pronouncing identity and favor over His disciples and listeners.

The word "peace" would have been a well-known word in Jesus' time. The Romans claimed it and the Jews prayed for it. For thousands of years shalom, the Hebrew word for peace, has been used to greet others and to bear them farewell. In a world of fragmentation and heightened anxiety, people have intentionally chosen to speak the word shalom over friends and strangers.

In the Beatitudes, Jesus speaks a few blessings, and as He does so, He chooses to incorporate the word "peace." Rather than the normal greeting of shalom. Jesus chooses to use a different phrase as He pronounced blessing and favor over His audience. He chooses to use the word, "peacemaker."

COREOLOGY

Principle #4, I will strive to become a peacemaker.

Now, think about this, Jesus's audience is made up of His disciples, as well as people He just healed. Read the last few verses of Matthew 4. To be ill and demon-possessed most likely carried significant social consequences for these people. They were thought to be unclean. The thinking of the day was that either they had sinned or their parents had sinned. Whatever the case, the belief was that the favor of God was not on them. It may have been years since someone had called them "Blessed." They had most likely experienced countless sleepless, restless nights far from the feeling of inner-peace or a peace from God.

Then, Jesus enters into their lives; the master at invitation, belonging, and ushering peace into human existence. As Jesus so graciously blesses people with words like meek, mourning, hungering for righteousness, and pure in heart, He surprisingly offers up a blessing about peace. Yet, instead of stating, "Blessed are those who have peace," or, "Blessed are those who champion peace," Jesus said, "Blessed are the peacemakers."

Principle 4: Peacemaking

In the Greek, it's the word eirēnopoioi, and it is to endeavor to reconcile persons who have disagreements. It's an active word. It's not a belief in the idea, but recognition that something needs to be built, made, and constructed. Jesus is either recognizing who the people currently are, or He is speaking peacemaking into existence. Either way, it is a radical statement that involves time, patience, strategy, and effort.

Of all the Beatitudes, this is the one that comes with a specific name and identity, "Blessed are the peacemakers, *for they will be called children of God.*" It's like Jesus is saying, "In this family, we work with God to promote the heart of God."

The Beatitudes aren't suggestions. When it comes to the ten commandments, God didn't ask His people to aim for a 70% success rate. When it comes to the fruit of the Spirit in Galatians 5, we're not asked to pick the five of the nine we care to embody. Similarly, with the beatitudes, Jesus doesn't offer up eight beatitudes and ask us to choose our favorites. Jesus is reshaping human hearts. It's not an all-or-nothing, but it is an all-are-to-be-embodied.

COREOLOGY

Jesus was thoughtful and strategic. Peacemaking is what He said, because peacemaking is what He was after.

And maybe He still is.

***

How can we cultivate peace in a world of fragmentation?

Is there a country or a political party in our world today that views peacemaking as an essential component of national security, economic stability, or foreign policy? It's not the rally cry used for anyone running for public office, yet I wonder how many of our churches see it as motivation that comes to us from the center of the heart of God.

When you live in a world obsessed with winning, peacemaking doesn't have a seat at the table. I think we all know that to unite a group of people, you need a rallying cry, but you also need a common enemy, or at least a common opponent. We rally to defeat our opponents, not to make peace with them.

Principle 4: Peacemaking

Philip Kenneson writes that when this happens, "We find ourselves offering not an alternate vision of how God would have us live together that is rooted in God's peace and wholeness, but merely a legislative agenda we would like to see advanced that would make us feel more at home in society."[21]

***

I began working on this chapter during Advent, just a few days before Christmas. As I reflected on what Bethlehem was like for Joseph and Mary, my heart was also heavy considering what Bethlehem was like this past Christmas. We sing about peace and silent nights every Christmas season, while also knowing that Joseph and Mary were away from home surrounded by animals. It's not the setting most women dream about when they think about the birth of their first child. You also had King Herod who had made a habit of sentencing people to death. Can you imagine the

---

[21] Philip Kenneson, *Life On the Vine*. Downers Grove, IL: InterVarsity Press, 1999), 95-96.

COREOLOGY

uncertainty and anxiety hovering over Joseph and Mary?
This past Christmas, as the war between Israel and Hamas carried on, I thought about the friends I have made in Jerusalem, Nazareth, and Bethlehem over the past few years. I thought about their families, jobs, and emotional well-being. I pray for peace, yet I find myself reflecting on what peace in that part of the world even looks like.

Cease-fire. You hear world leaders, including President Biden, promoting cease-fire between Israel and Palestine. It's a strategy calling for a temporary halt to military invasion and strategic action. It's a pause. People take a break. For a few weeks, people can breathe a little better. Yet, everyone knows it is temporary. It's not an end to war. Much like Ross and Rachel on *Friends*, they take a break.

My assumption is that when many of us think about peacemaking, what's really on our minds is cease-fire. And they're not the same. A cease-fire is a pause knowing that conflict will return in the future. Peacemaking is the commitment to work to a better future. Ceasefire doesn't change how one side feels about the other. In fact, it may grow the resentment.

Principle 4: Peacemaking

Peacemaking is meant to turn the opponent into a companion. A ceasefire doesn't involve interaction between two or more sides. Peacemaking can't happen without people coming together. A ceasefire doesn't involve a table. Peacemaking has at the center, a table.

***

Someone once said that when all you care about is wins and losses, all you are left with are casualties. Peacemaking doesn't mean you don't have convictions, but that you refuse to let your convictions keep you from the false belief that those who don't have your same convictions are the enemy, or even worse, that they aren't cared for by God. We know we have made God in our own image when God loves and hates all the same people we do.

A world leader once said, "Thus, I believe that I am acting in accordance with the will of the Almighty Creator."

Especially, for believers in Jesus, statements like this pique our interest. We are drawn to leaders who are led by their faith. Yet, how often have we witnessed

COREOLOGY

leaders (in politics and the church), use statements about faith in God to promote their worldly agenda. The world leader whom I just quoted also said, "By defending myself against the Jew, I am fighting for the work of the Lord." Unfortunately, millions of his followers not only listened to him, but bought into the same way of seeing the world.

That world leader was Adolf Hitler.[22] We know how that story goes.

Ed Stetzer writes, "You can't hate people and engage them with the gospel at the same time. You can't war with people and show the love of Jesus. You can't be both outraged and on mission."[23]

I think Ed is right. I also think that many Christians think that peacemaking is equal to not hating people. Jesus doesn't call us to a gospel of tolerance or

---

[22] Adolf Hitler, *Mein Kampf*.

[23] Ed Stetzer, *Christians in the Age of Outrage: How to Bring Our Best When the World Is at Its Worst* (Carol Stream, IL: Tyndale, 2018), 105.

Principle 4: Peacemaking

cordiality, but to a mission of peacemaking. And this takes work.
New Testament authors carry on this rally cry of peace. Soak these in:

Romans 14:19, "Let us therefore make every effort to do what leads to *peace* and to mutual edification."

John 14:27, "*Peace* I leave with you; my *peace* I give you. I do not give to you as the world gives. Do not let your hearts be troubled and do not be afraid."

Colossians 3:15, "Let the *peace* of Christ rule in your hearts, since as members of one body you were called to *peace*."

James 3:18, "*Peacemakers* who sow in *peace* reap a harvest of righteousness."

Colossians 1:19-20, "For God was pleased to have all His fullness dwell in Him, and through Him to reconcile to Himself all things, whether things on earth or things

in heaven, by *making peace* through His blood, shed on the cross.

COREOLOGY

If God has established peace by reconciling us to Him through the cross, then we must do all we can to embody this reality as well.

***

There are many faith traditions who take communion every week. Some may call it the Eucharist, the Lord's Table, or the Lord's Supper. It's the communal sharing of the bread and cup that represents the body and blood of Christ. There are faith traditions who exchange these words every week as they share the bread and cup, "The peace of Christ."

It's only four words, but they carry so much weight. It's a reminder that at the cross, Jesus had peace and peacemaking in mind. We remember that when Jesus rose from the grave and met with His disciples in John 20, the first phrase He spoke was, "Peace be with you." The peace of Christ is something we inhale and exhale. We digest so that we can extend it to the world.

This kind of peace is so much more than a feeling or a lofty idea.

Principle 4: Peacemaking

Sure, the Romans championed Pax Romana, the peace of Rome. Yes, Caesar promised peace. Yet, the motto and promise of peace was yours to have as long as you abided by Rome's standards. However, Jesus delivered on peace. He delivers on it, promises it, and tasks us to go out and make it. He hasn't given up on peace's potential. Neither should we.

For peace to rule in hearts (as Colossians 1:15 states), it's vitally important that we examine where peace is not present in us, name it for what it is, and develop daily rhythms to allow God to work His transforming power.

Let me help you. Take five minutes each day to dwell on the verses shared in this chapter. Write them on an index card or save them in the notes on your phone. Ask God to reveal the places in your heart that are resistant to peace. Write down what comes to mind. Ask God to fill you with the peace that abides in Christ. Open your hands as you pray. I have found in my life that my heart often follows where my posture takes it.

As for peacemaking, it doesn't mean complete reconciliation. There may be severed relationships in your life that need healing, but that doesn't mean

COREOLOGY

they need to go back to what they once were. It does mean that you need to do the hard work of getting rid of anger, bitterness, and resentment that are clogging up the arteries from God's peace dwelling in your heart.

Peacemaking often works best when practiced in community. Gather with a few friends, focus on Matthew 5:9, and pray for God to give your group tangible next steps.

***

Barbara Brown Taylor, one of my favorite preachers and authors, once challenged people to occasionally consider taking the bread and the cup to the sidewalks of your church building, instead of sharing the elements inside facing the stage. Her challenge wasn't an indictment on how many of us receive communion. She simply wanted people to think about the implications of sharing in Christ. On the sidewalks, with your brothers and sisters in Christ, sharing the bread and the cup, we're reminded that this is more than an individual, private moment with God, but that the bread and the cup calls us to be something in the world, and for the world.

Principle 4: Peacemaking

The peace of Christ.

Received through Christ.

Now, go and make it in the world.

Chapter 5

Principle #5: I will practice <u>hospitality</u> as a way to learn, grow, and invest in other people.

The 2016 presidential election campaign was hostile. A lot of people were wounded and scarred after it was all over. Some relatives weren't talking to each other. Lines were drawn. Anger turned into deep forms of resentment. For some, whatever interest they had in politics was lost, while for others, it whet their appetite for more.

As culture wars continue to drive wedges between humans, some people are choosing to do something about it. After the 2016 election season, three marriage and family therapists decided to launch an effort to get folks talking to each other again. It was a risk. But they were able to find ten Trump and eleven

COREOLOGY

Clinton supporters to come together for conversation. Their deep hope was to depolarize America. Talk about an ambitious dream. As they gathered for a meal and dialogue, they realized they had things in common.

The group set out with three goals: one, try to understand the other side's point of view, even if there is disagreement. Two, engage those you disagree with and look for common ground with ways to work together. And three, especially in politics, support principles that bring you together, rather than divide you.

The group has a name, *Better Angels*, and they now host around two dozen gatherings a month nationwide. Do they solve all the world's problems? No. But they do discover that disagreeing on certain issues doesn't have to keep humans from kindness, friendship, and progress.

I think it's safe to say that *Better Angels* would not have the same success if they attempted to generate online dialogue among Trump and Clinton supporters. Put them all on zoom together, and it still might be

Principle 5: Hospitality

difficult to find common ground and unite around common goals.
There is something about the dinner table, that opens up the heart to engage in meaningful dialogue. It's hard to think of another setting in the world that provides the same space and opportunity.

I think the local church should be the place where people can talk about anything. Now, this doesn't mean the stage (or platform) is the place for the conversation. It could be small groups, Bible classes, or intentional environments created for meaningful dialogue. There should be no issue or topic that the church can't provide space for as we attempt to navigate faith and culture. We would like to think that the waters of baptism and the bread and cup; hold the power to keep us united through it all.

***

Now, I think it is important that Jesus-followers commit to be Gospel-driven, not issue-driven. This is why it is essential that we develop principles in our lives that keep us rooted in the heart and mission of Jesus. Jesus is the center point. He is the core that equips us to be strong, healthy, and vibrant.

COREOLOGY

Conversations shouldn't drive us to the life and teachings of Jesus, as much as conversations should flow from the heart and mission of Jesus.

Without submitting to a Christ-centered life, we drift. When we're driving, it doesn't take much of a distraction to cause us to veer into another lane or onto rumble strips. Or think about it this way, have you ever been on a float in a swimming pool or on the lake? If you close your eyes for just a few minutes, you can slowly drift from the shore or side of the pool without even knowing it. Especially in seasons with heightened waves causing us to drift, we must stay connected to our anchor. It's not good enough to just be close to it, we must be connected to it.

The book of Hebrews speaks about drifting. Hebrews 2:1 says, "We must pay the most careful attention, therefore, to what we have heard, so that we do not drift away." There is a concern that people are drifting from the center. They haven't completely turned their back on the Gospel, they've just drifted from it. The author wants people to be properly rooted, which is why they come back to this image in Hebrews 6:19, "We have this hope as an anchor for the soul, firm and secure."

Principle 5: Hospitality

Let's stay in Hebrews for a moment, because the final chapter offers a few nuggets of wisdom as a way to encourage deep, meaningful connection. The final chapter begins with these two statements, "Keep on loving one another as brothers and sisters. Do not forget to show hospitality to strangers."

Principle #5, *I will practice hospitality as a way to learn, grow, and invest in other people.*

Hospitality is one of those things that sounds great, just please don't make us do it. In the Greek, hospitality is the word philoxenias. Philos means friend and xenos means stranger. Think about that. To be hospitable is to be a friend to a stranger. It's hard enough to open our homes for friends, much less for strangers, right?

When it comes to practicing hospitality, we can come up with countless reasons not to do it. The laundry never ends. The yard needs to be mowed. Family portraits have either not been hung or are outdated.

By in large, our homes have gotten larger while hospitality has declined.

COREOLOGY

I don't want to overburden you with this principle, so hang on with me for the ride. I want to broaden what hospitality can look like for you. I want to gently nudge you to consider the positive impact hospitality and table fellowship can have on your life and the world around you.

No one is going to argue that hospitality wasn't important in the early church. Paul promotes it in Romans 12:13, "Share with the Lord's people who are in need. Practice hospitality." Peter highlights it in 1 Peter 4:9, "Offer hospitality to one another without grumbling." Jesus stayed with strangers in Samaria for two days in John 4:40 and Peter took on ethnic barriers by staying in the home of a Roman centurion named Cornelius for several days in Acts 10:48.

I think for many of us, it's not a matter of hospitality being a good thing, it's just that we don't have much room for it in our lives.

Table and food fill the pages of Scripture. It is estimated that 70% of Jesus's parables involve food in some form. In Luke, it seems like Jesus is constantly going to a meal, enjoying a meal, or leaving a meal.

Principle 5: Hospitality

Name a close relationship in your life that hasn't grown because of eating together. We center friendship, marriages, small groups, and holidays around it. Christians all over the world share in the Lord's Table every week. Table and faith go hand in hand. Leonard Sweet says, "An untabled faith is an unstable faith."[24] Sure, hospitality can involve couches, chairs, and places to sleep, but the table may just be the most important component of hospitality.

Table fellowship is vital for healthy families. Sociologist Cody C. Delistraty presented research in the Atlantic Monthly discussing this:

- The #1 factor for parents raising kids who are drug-free, healthy, intelligent, kind human beings? Frequent family dinners.
- The #1 shaper of vocabulary in younger children, even more than any other family event, including play? Frequent family dinners.

---

[24] Leonard Sweet, *From Tablet to Table*. (Colorado Springs, CO: NavPress), 9.

COREOLOGY

- The #1 predictor of future academic success for elementary-age children? Frequent family dinners.
- The variable most associated with lower incidence of depressive and suicidal thoughts among 11–18-year-olds? Frequent family dinners.[25]

Are you surprised?

If frequent family dinners are that important for the nuclear family, consider how important it is for the family of God, the church. Relationships grow when we sit down at tables together.

Alan Hirsch and Lance Ford say it like this, "If every Christian family in the world simply offered good conversational hospitality around a table once a week to neighbors, we could eat our way into the Kingdom of God."[26]

---

[25] Leonard Sweet, *From Tablet to Table*. (Colorado Springs, CO: NavPress), 12.

[26] Alan Hirsch and Lance Ford, *Right Here, Right Now: Everyday Mission for Everyday People* (Grand Rapids: MI: Baker Books, 2011), 51.

Principle 5: Hospitality

Our staff at Sycamore View does this every week. A normal Monday includes a staff meeting at 10am and a staff lunch immediately following. We began this over a decade ago. We wanted our staff meeting to be focused on spiritual formation, communication, events, mission, and celebration. We began eating lunch together as a space to tell stories, share our lives, laugh, catch up, and enjoy each other's company. For some, it may seem like a waste of time. For us, it has led to deeper bonds, trust, love, and appreciation for our teammates. There are things we need to do in meetings that we don't want to do at lunch. And there are things we do at lunch that we don't want to do in meetings. When we miss a week or two of staff lunch, we feel it.

***

Table fellowship as hospitality is made easier when we're with friends, but what about strangers, neighbors, and those we don't know very well? Is it worth the risk? Is it possible?

In many ways, we live in a scary world. It was reported that in the first few weeks of 2024, Memphis is averaging forty-four stolen vehicles per day. That's not

COREOLOGY

forty-four cars being broken into, but stolen. Walking into shopping malls can take some courage. Mass shootings have become far too normal. And don't even get me started on all the crazy drivers in the world.

It's hard enough to trust people you know well, much less strangers and neighbors we barely know.

Unfortunately, our world has messed up the way we think. Do we see people as a gift to the world? Or do we see them as a threat to the world?

Harvard psychologist Mina Cikara wrote that when you start fearing others, "Your circle of who you counted as friends is going to shrink. And that means those people outside of your bounds get less empathy, get fewer resources."[27] Think about how this plays out in politics, national security, and even in friendships. We gravitate to the people, and the groups of people, that make us feel the most safe and

---

[27] Mina Cikara, quoted in Brian Resnick, "What Brexit Can Teach Us About the Psychology of Fear," Vox, June 25, 2016, www.vox.come/2016/6/25/12023768/brexit-psychology-fear.

Principle 5: Hospitality

comfortable. There is psychological ease in being surrounded by similar people.

There was a study done on social networks (not social media network, but friends you'd discuss life with). What they found is that for 75% of white people, their network is 100% white. For 65% of black people, 100% are black. For Latinos, 50% of their network is 100% Latino. Of one-hundred friends a person may have, the average white person has 91 white friends, and the average black person has 83 black friends.[28] This simply shows that it's difficult to break through cultural and social barriers.

Needless to say, we have challenges in front of us. But in the Kingdom of God, challenges are opportunities. "Our biggest fear," writes Krish Kandiah in *God as Stranger*, "may turn out to be our greatest opportunity."[29]

---

[28] Daniel Cox, Juhem Navarrow-Rivera, and Robert P. Jones, "Race, Religion, and Political Affiliation of Americans' Core Social Networks," Public Religion Research Institute, August 3, 2016, www.prri.org/research/poll-race-religion-politics-americans-social-networks/.

[29] Krish Kandiah, *God is Stranger*.

COREOLOGY

Henri Nouwen wrote, "Our society seems to be increasingly full of fearful, defensive, aggressive people anxiously clinging to their property and inclined to look at their surrounding world with suspicion, always expecting an enemy to suddenly appear, intrude and do harm. But still—that is our vocation: to convert the enemy into a guest and to create the free and fearless space where brotherhood and sisterhood can be formed and fully experienced."[30]

***

I have two friends. Ok, I think I have lot more friends than two, but the two friends I'm referring to didn't know each other, but they were Facebook friends. There was a sensitive, cultural issue being discussed online and these two friends ended up in the same comment section. This is a scary place to be. As I've said before, online comment sections are often where Christian-witness goes to die. But this day, one friend invited the other to lunch. They were polar opposites in so many ways, yet, they went to lunch to share their hearts instead of going after each other online for all to see. They left lunch without convincing the other

---

[30] Henri Nouwen, *Reaching Out: The Three Movements of the Spiritual Life* (New York: Image Books, 1986), 65-66.

Principle 5: Hospitality

about their conviction concerning the issue, but they also left as friends.

In the Kingdom of God, tables > comment sections.

"Hospitality is the act or process whereby the identity of the stranger is transformed into that of guest," writes Jipp, "the primary impulse of hospitality is to create a safe and welcoming place where a stranger can be converted into a friend."[31] And I want us to believe that this is possible.

***

Many stories have been told about Magic Johnson and Larry Bird. They were rivals in college and as professionals they often battled each other for championships. One year, Converse signed them to shoe deals, and a commercial was scheduled to be filmed on Larry Bird's farm.

---

[31] Joshua W. Jipp, *Saved by Faith and Hospitality* (Grand Rapids, MI: Eerdmans, 2017), 22.

COREOLOGY

After filming a portion of the commercial, they broke for lunch. Magic was walking off the set when Larry's mother called out from their porch, "Magic, you're eating with us today." Magic may have been able to tell Larry no, but he couldn't resist Larry's mother. They sat at a table, and they ate. Later Larry would say that at lunch that day, Magic Johnson became Earvin Johnson. Their friendship only grew from that day forward. It's amazing what a table can do.

***

We need more tables, not less of them. We have the time. Will we take the risk? In a weird way, tables are a healing agent. In *The Divine Commodity*, Skye Jethani writes, "The English word *hospitality* originates from the same Latin root word as the word *hospital*. A hospital is literally a 'home for strangers.' Of course, it has come to mean a place of healing. There is a link between being welcomed and being healed. Our homes are hospitals—refuges of healing radiating the light of heaven. And our dinner tables are to be operating tables—the place where broken souls are made whole again. . . when we lower our defenses, when we remove our facades and our peepholes, and

Principle 5: Hospitality

we begin to be truly present with one another—then the healing power of the gospel can begin its work."[32]

Take the risk. Expand your table. You have more to offer to the world than you think. You have more to receive from the world than you think. What do you have to lose?

As a Kingdom person, choose the table over the comment section. At tables, defenses can come crashing down. Healing occurs. You may not leave in total agreement on every issue our world presents to us, but you can leave knowing you're on the same team with the person you ate with.

The Kingdom of God is asking for risk-takers when it comes to hospitality and the table.

Go for it.
Give it a shot.
And see what God might do.

---

[32] Skye Jethani, *The Divine Commodity: Discovering a Faith Beyond Consumer Christianity* (Grand Rapids, MI: Zondervan, 2009), 153-54.

Chapter 6

Principle #6: I will choose to regularly <u>serve</u> others.

Jesus is on the record saying things like, "But many who are first will be last, and many who are last will be first."[33] Did he mean it? Or was He simply trying to nudge people to prioritize their relationship with God?

On another occasion when He was pressured to promise permanent seats of honor in His future Kingdom to two apostles, Jesus responded, "Instead, whoever wants to become great among you must be your servant, and whoever wants to be first must be

---

[33] Matthew 19:30.

COREOLOGY

your slave."[34] Was Jesus really rejecting their request and giving them a vision of service instead?

A few days before His death, Jesus painted a vivid picture of the hungry being fed, the thirsty receiving a drink, the stranger being welcomed, the naked being clothed, the sick receiving care, and the imprisoned receiving visitors. He ended the story by challenging His listeners, "The King will reply, 'Truly I tell you, whatever you did for one of the least of these brothers and sisters of mine, you did for me.'"[35] Was He being literal? Or just trying to make a point?

For Jesus, service was to become such a natural way of life for His followers, that you wouldn't even have to think about doing it. And the motivation to live a life of service was not to gain a reward or to elevate status, but because it's the Jesus way to live. Jesus didn't just teach about living a life of service, He modeled it.

---

[34] Matthew 20:26.

[35] Matthew 25:40-45.

Principle 6: Service

When it comes to service, Jesus sets the bar high.

Principle #6: *I will choose to regularly serve others.*

***

Way back in the fourth century, a plague hit the region of Caesarea. There wasn't an understanding of germs, hygiene, and vaccinations, so plagues were catastrophic and, in many ways, unstoppable.

If you had resources, you fled. You got out of town. You took off to the countryside. Yet, it wasn't unusual for one group of people to stay behind, the Christians. Compelled by their devotion to Jesus, they stayed back to put into practice His way of life.

Their actions did not go unnoticed. The local bishop, Eusebius, was also an historian, and he wrote, "All day long some of them (the Christians) tended to the dying and to their burial, countless numbers with no one to care for them. Others gathered from all parts of the city a multitude of those withered from famine and distributed bread to them all."[36] You don't do

COREOLOGY

these kinds of things unless you have sworn your allegiance to a different King and Kingdom. Jesus had won their hearts.

Not too long after Eusebius wrote about the compassionate lives of Christ-followers, there was an Emperor named Julian who also took notice of the actions of this group of people. Julian was a military leader, a philosopher, an author, and the nephew of Constantine the Great. At one point he wrote to pagan priests encouraging them to imitate the charity modeled by Christians. Think about that. A pagan Emperor wanted his pagan priests to behave more like Christians because of the good they brought to the world.

Writing to a pagan priest, Emperor Julian wrote, "They (the Christians) support not only their poor, but ours as well, all men see that our people lack aid from us."[37]

---

[36] https://biblemesh.com/blog/the-compassion-of-early-christians/.

[37] Julian, *Fragment of a Letter to a Priest,* 337, in *The Works of the Emperor Julian,* translated by Wilmer Cave Wright (New York: The MacMillan Co., 1913).

Principle 6: Service

Throughout the centuries, there have been plenty of times when Christians have failed miserably to uphold the values and actions of Christ, yet there have also been countless times Christians have gotten it right.

So, what about now? Would pagan leaders, or non-Christians for that matter, observe the actions and behaviors of Christians and write, "That group of people love, serve, and care for others without limits. For them, service isn't about handing out turkeys once a year. They just keep showing up."

***

People who choose service as a way of life will experience rejection, being taken advantage of, and burnout, which present challenges to keep a heart soft. Hard and calloused hearts don't make for faithful servant hearts. I'm interested in how we keep our hearts soft.

Soft hearts are moldable. Hard hearts are not.

Soft hearts are open hearts. Hard hearts are closed.

COREOLOGY

Soft hearts are open to God. Hard hearts leave little room for God.
Soft hearts see all people as image-bearers of God. Hard hearts see the world as us vs them.

Soft hearts want to be a part of the good in the world even though they know plenty of evil exists. Hard hearts disengage from the world because they see it as a threat.

Soft hearts make room for God and people. Hard hearts do not.

***

On January 21, 2018, my family left church to meet some friends at Central BBQ for lunch. The Ross family thoroughly enjoys sharing life and talking faith over a sausage and cheese plate, BBQ nachos, and a rack of ribs. As our food was being delivered, Kayci received a call from Alarm Alert that they detected a broken window at our home. They asked if we would like to dispatch the police. We said yes.

Our food had just arrived, but I knew I needed to run home to check on everything. I thought I'd get a laugh

Principle 6: Service

in before I left, so I looked at Kayci and said, "Do you mind driving home really quick to check on everything?" I had some food to devour. Don't get in between a preacher and their Sunday lunch. I left trusting that they would leave me food to eat.

I drove up to our home expecting to find that everything was fine and that it was a false alarm, but I noticed in the back of the house that a window had been broken. Sure enough, we had been broken into. It's somewhat humorous that most stories pastors have of being broken into either happen during a Sunday worship service or a funeral.

The police arrived and walked through the home to make sure no one was still inside. Our two televisions were gone. That was all the thieves took from us. They broke a window and took our televisions. But if you have ever been broken into before, you know that the feeling of being violated can eat away at your heart.

We had moved into our neighborhood with compassion and service in mind. We desperately wanted to neighbor well. Our neighbors protected and cared for us, and we protected and care for them. That morning, most of our neighbors were at church

COREOLOGY

too. My concern was that this event would damage Kayci, Truitt, and Noah's hearts.

About an hour later, my family arrived. I didn't know what to expect. Truitt was the first one through the door, "Dad-e-o! What's going on man? I hear we got robbed. Tell me pops, where are we going to watch NFL playoff games today? A friend's house? Want to borrow a tv? My vote is Buffalo Wild Wings!"

Based on his demeanor, I figured Truitt was doing ok with the news.

Noah walked in with revenge on his mind, "Dad! Here's what we're going to do. You and I are going to go find whoever did this. You're going to grab them, throw them on the ground, and then I'm going to kick them."

Though he was angry, he seemed to be ok.

Kayci walked in with a smile on her face. She gave me a big hug. I was two days away from traveling to Africa with Compassion International. She leaned her head back though her arms were still around me, "Josh, we're going to be just fine. You're going to Africa."

Principle 6: Service

I said, "Kayci, no I'm not. I leave in two days, and we have a broken window at our home."
She said, "Listen, you step up in front of our church every week and talk about how we are called by God to be bold and courageous and to not live in fear. Now, you need to live that out."

I quickly responded, "Baby, don't be using my words against me."

Our home was fine. My family was fine. I went to Africa. I also ate the BBQ my family so graciously boxed up and brought home to me.

But I had some decisions to make about my heart. I knew that it was going to take work to keep it soft.

***

I am convinced that it takes time for a heart to grow hard. An event can set it in motion, but a heart doesn't grow hard overnight. It's like the slow drip of an IV.

I am also convinced that it takes even longer for a hard heart to become soft again.

COREOLOGY

Thankfully, after our break-in, I pressed into spiritual disciplines and therapy to ensure that I would not allow my heart to become hard toward God or people. Maintaining a regular practice of service became a vital part of my journey. I didn't need forms of service in my life because I wanted a reward, but because it is through service that God teaches me so much about His heart and life.

I've shared about our break-in and keeping our hearts soft in multiple settings before and it's a message that has resonated with people who have experienced forms of trauma. It connects with police officers who often see the worst of our cities. It has opened doors for meaningful conversations with social workers and non-profit leaders. In a world where darkness is at work to made hearts hard, God is at work to keep hearts soft.

***

Heightened political seasons carry the power to harden hearts. The fear-based messaging and demonization of opponents is like that slow drip of an IV, and if we aren't intentional, we become people we never desired to be. Hearts can become hard, and

Principle 6: Service

when they become hard, it's difficult to receive and extend love.

Andy Stanley reminds us, "Our first-, second-, and third-century brothers and sisters captured the attention of their pagan neighbors through their character, morality, work ethic, and friendship."[38]

While encouraging Christians to lead quiet lives, Paul always had witness to the world in mind. He cared about behaving properly toward outsiders. He commanded that leaders in churches have positive reputations in their communities. They could only do this by allowing their hearts to stay soft in God.

There is some truth to the meme that has been floating around social media addressed to those of us living in the United States, "If Paul were alive today, we'd be getting a letter." His letter would remind us that Jesus didn't die and rise again for people to submit to a party, a leader, or a political agenda, but to the Kingdom that is above every Kingdom. Again,

---

[38] Andy Stanley, *Not In It to Win It*. (Grand Rapids, MI: Zondervan, 2022), 101.

COREOLOGY

Stanley writes, "Early Christians were not despised for their behavior. They were despised by the empire for their allegiance to Christ...I'm not suggesting that you love your country less. I'm suggesting that we love one another better."[39]

Don't you want that?

***

Imagine if service becomes a regular part of our lives. Don't you know it will help us to envision a world that is bigger than our own little story?

Lives of service have always been one of the most noticeable ways to show that our hearts have been given over to Jesus. By lives of service, I'm referring to the intentional things we do: volunteering with non-profits, feeding the hungry, or tutoring children at the local school. We have the time, will we make it a priority?

---

[39] Andy Stanley, *Not In It to Win It*. (Grand Rapids, MI: Zondervan, 2022), 102.

Principle 6: Service

There are also the things we do because it has become a part of our lives: holding doors, moving the neighbor's trash can, paying for a stranger's meal, picking up trash, and returning shopping carts at the grocery store.

Service reminds us that we are a part of a bigger story than ourselves.

Service is an overflow of God's love for us. We don't serve in order for God to love us, but because He loves us.

Service is at the core of the heart and mission of Jesus, and it is only right that it is a major, consistent part of our lives too.

Be creative. Be intentional. Be spontaneous. Be faithful in the small things.

FINAL WORDS

By the grace of God, I have now been pastoring in a local church since 2003. This means I have preached through five presidential election seasons. They are exhausting. But they don't have to be.

I did my best to write with a pastoral voice, not a prophetic voice. My intentions are to remind people of the calling God has placed on us. We are being shaped and formed by events and voices all around us, which means we must give careful attention how we are allowing Jesus to shape and form us into the kinds of people God wants us to be.

So, imagine with me.

Imagine if followers of Jesus diligently decided to take seriously our confession that Jesus is the Lord of our

COREOLOGY

lives and nothing else is. How could we not live with greater loyalty and passion?

Imagine if Jesus-followers were to create and honor spiritual practices that keep us rooted in God. Can't you envision how we could live greater peace and meaning?

Imagine if we refuse to allow media outlets to have a loud voice in our lives. Don't you know fear and anger would have a difficult time growing in us?

Imagine if we accept the challenge to be peacemakers. Are you able to see the role we could play in bringing God's healing to this world?

Imagine if hospitality were to replace the internet as the primary place for conversations about what is happening in the world. Do you see how it can bring us together?

Imagine if service becomes a regular part of our lives. Can't you see how hard it is for hatred to grow where love thrives?

Let's be intentional, especially in election seasons, to live in a way that we will like who we are when the elections are over.

Care about the world. Be educated about issues and policies. Vote if you feel the need to.

But do not give your heart to any other leader or kingdom.

Your spiritual core will not be strengthened by accident. Grow in God. Grow with God. Grow for God.

Guard your heart.

Protect your joy.

Don't lose your Kingdom-witness.

You can do this.

We can do this.

God can do this in us.

Acknowledgements

Kayci, I told you the night before we got married that after being a child of God and a disciple of Jesus, there is not a title I wear with more pride than being your husband. I still believe that. Thank you for believing in me.

Truitt and Noah, I hope this book can play a part in helping you embrace a deep love for Jesus while believing that you have so much to offer to this world. Be courageous, brave, and bold. Do not give into all the fear tactics that come your way.

Mom and dad, thank you for raising me to be a risk-taker.

Jonathan, I treasure the one-on-one time we have together to process life.

Luke, Josh, Chris, Mike, and Rick, you guys are a gift to my life. Todd, Krista, Justin, Ashley, Brad, and Amy, you are our safe place. I can't imagine life without you.

COREOLOGY

Troy Robertson, our conversations about faith and culture encourage and inspire me.

Michael Boykin, thank you for all the ways you genuinely care for me and my family. You are a loyal friend and a great encourager.

Sycamore View Church, let's keep helping people see Jesus together. Sycamore View Staff, I love what we have together. Sycamore View shepherds, thank you for believing in me.

Jenna King, thank you for your partnership in helping this book come to life. I am appreciative of your attention to detail. Even more than you editing this book, thank you for the role you play at Harding Academy to pastor my kids and the entire school.

Glenn Hailey, you and I may be thirty-seven years apart, but you've become a dear friend. We do not always see the world the same way, but the depth of our friendship transcends our few differences. Thank you for loving me and my family so well.

David and Theresa, you embody the heartbeat of this book. I love you both!

APPENDIX

In chapter 2, we discussed why consistent spiritual practices are essential to our health, maturity, and growth. In many Christian circles, one way to live into spiritual practices is to develop a Rule of Life. A rule of life "is simply a pattern of attitudes, behaviors, and practices that are regular and routine and are intended to produce a certain quality of life and character in us."[40]

Here are a few resources to consider:

- Ruth Haley Barton, *Strengthening the Soul of Your Leadership*, with a focus on chapter 8.
- Marjorie Thompson, *Soul Feast*, with a focus on chapter 9.
- John Mark Comer, *Practicing the Way*.

---

[40] Ruth Haley Barton, *Strengthening the Soul of Your Leadership*. (Downers Grove, IL: InterVarsity Press, 2018), 128.

Made in the USA
Middletown, DE
05 October 2024